# The Complete Diabetic Cookbook

*The Diabetes Weight Loss Book with Healthy and Delicious Recipes For Every Day incl. 30 Days Weight Loss Plan*

[1st Edition]

**Kate Miller**

TABLE OF CONTENTS

## What is diabetes?

Diabetes is the name for a disease in the body in where the bloody contains too much glucose. An excess of blood glucose can be caused by several factors. The pancreas (an organ in the body) is responsible for producing insulin, which is a hormone that helps glucose be absorbed from the bloodstream into cells for conversion into energy. When the body is incapable of producing enough or any insulin at all, this can cause a type of diabetes. Another type of diabetes is caused by the body not being able to use the insulin that the body makes, which will also lead to an excess of glucose in the bloodstream. Over a long term, too much glucose in the bloodstream can lead to a number of different health problems. Diabetes is a serious disease, and unfortunately incurable. However, diabetes is treatable with medication and lifestyle adjustments, and people with diabetes can expect to live long and healthy lives with a proper management plan. Because people with diabetes are required to closely monitor their blood sugar levels and can sometimes struggle to keep them in check, losing weight as a diabetic can be challenging. However, it is not impossible, and this book will outline some strategies for maintaining a healthy lifestyle geared towards losing weight.

## Differences between Type I and Type II diabetes

Diabetes has two main types found in society. These two types have different causes, but essentially lead to the same conclusion of too much glucose in the blood. Knowing which type you have is important in creating and following a proper treatment plan, as the medication will differ in order to counter the effects of the disease. Here are the main differences between the two types.

Type I–This type is caused by the body not being able to produce insulin (either at all or in large enough quantities) to lower or control the body's blood sugar levels. This type of diabetes is usually present at birth and diagnosed in early childhood. Type I diabetes is an autoimmune disease, which means that the body attacks its own insulin-making cells at the detriment of itself. No one knows why it is caused. Type I diabetes is normally treated by insulin injections, either through individual injections or through a pump. People who are Type I diabetics can never come off their medication; there is no cure for type 1 diabetes.

Type II–Type II diabetes is caused when the body does not accept or use the insulin it produces to diminish glucose levels in the body and to absorb glucose properly. When the body develops this condition, titled "insulin resistance", the body pushes itself to produce more and more insulin to make up for the resistance. This can eventually burn out the insulin producing cells, called beta cells. Type II diabetes is often associated with excessive weight and obesity, as the excess weight that the body carries will affect the body's sensitivity to insulin. Type II, depending on the situation, can be treated by medications that increase the body's sensitivity to the existing insulin in the body, or by extra added insulin injections to compensate for the body's burnt out beta cells. Some people with type II diabetes are eventually able to go off medication with the proper diet and lifestyle adjustments, but many type II diabetics are on medications for life.

This table highlights the main differences between type I and II diabetes:

| Type I | Type II |
|---|---|
| Little or no insulin production | Some insulin production (may be inefficient) |
| Body attacks own beta cells | Body builds up resistance to insulin, putting strain on beta cells |
| Treated by insulin injections | Treated by medications and sometimes insulin injections |
| Diagnosed early (childhood) | Diagnosed later (childhood – old age) |

# Prevention Measures

Type I diabetes is unpreventable. People who have type I diabetes are born with it, and there is little to no understanding of what causes it. However, type II diabetes can often be prevented through simple lifestyle changes and precautionary measures. People who have a parent or sibling with type II diabetes are more likely to develop it later in their lives. The same goes for people with gestational diabetes (which occurs during pregnancy for people with uteri) and who are overweight. However, almost anyone can prevent or delay type II diabetes by doing some of the following things:

*Losing Weight Effectively* – People who are overweight can prevent or delay diabetes by losing a healthy amount of weight and then keeping it off. If weight loss is done in a healthy and long-term manner, this prevention measure can prevent diabetes and a host of other problems such as high blood pressure, high cholesterol and other related issues. The key to this prevention measure is approaching this solution with a plan that takes baby steps. Drastic lifestyle changes can be ineffective, unhealthy and frustrating.

*Exercising Regularly* – 30 minutes of aerobic exercise are recommended for a healthy adult. This can be achieved by walking daily or incorporating another type of reasonable exercise into your daily routine as a part of your daily self-care routine. If you do not enjoy high-intensity exercises like jogging or aerobics classes, other options that are safer on the joints include water aerobics, swimming laps, using an elliptical machine or taking a dance class. With the variety of classes, groups of interest and styles of working out available these days, there is an option for every type of person and for every preference.

*Eating Healthily* – A healthy diet directly relates to the body's ability to prevent or delay diabetes. A healthy diet should be well-rounded and include a variety of grains, fruits, vegetables and protein sources every day. While highly processed foods are readily available and enjoyable to each, these should not make up the majority of your diet. The ideal mindset when trying to achieve a healthy lifestyle, is moderation. Everyone should enjoy the treats they love, but not at the sacrifice of their bodily health. Every diet should be balanced with a healthy distribution of carbohydrates, fats and proteins. A typical ratio for these macronutrients is 50%, 20% and 30% respectively. There are many apps and websites that help people calculate the right number of macronutrients for their activity level and specific needs. (Continue this)

## Diabetes and Food: Where do I have to pay attention?

Diabetics should avoid foods that cause their blood sugars to spike too rapidly, and especially need to make sure they are incorporating a wide variety of foods into their daily diet. For diabetics who want to lose weight, there are some areas of food that should be avoided. However, note this disclaimer that says that anything in moderation is okay. You should not deprive yourself of any food forever. Moderation and a sustainable lifestyle are much healthier and more achievable than any sort of crash diet. With that in mind, here are some areas to keep a close eye on:

*Sugars*- all types of added sugars are more detrimental to people with diabetes. This is because the high amount of glucose already existing in these foods can cause blood sugar levels to spike quickly, which is not healthy for people with type II diabetes. Any added sugars or natural sugars like agave, honey, molasses, granulated sugar or maple syrup should be avoided in large quantities. The only real exception to this is fruit.

*Sweetened Drinks* – for the same reasons above, any drinks with added sugars like sodas, some fruit juices, sweet tea and sweetened coffee drinks should be avoided. Instead, opt for unsweetened versions of these drinks, like flavored seltzer water, iced tea with fruit flavors, coffee with 2% and all natural fruit juice. Do not opt for diet sodas as the aspartame in these drinks is not good for the body either.

*Highly Processed Foods* – processed junk foods like chips, fried foods, pastry snacks, cookies and candy offers little to no nutritional value at a high calorie cost. For anyone looking to lose weight, this food offers little value other than a quick moment of good taste. Avoid these foods, and instead, pick snacks that contain a strong protein or fiber base, that will fill you up and allow you to stay energized for longer.

*Sauces/Condiments* – watch what types of sauces and condiments you choose to put on your foods. Many sauces and condiments have an overload of hidden added sugars, which may not be readily observed. Make sure you read the nutritional labels of your typical condiments and be ready to adjust for your diet's sake.

*Alcohol* – while a drink in moderation is okay, alcohol is notoriously high in empty calories. Drinks like beer and wine have the same caloric value as many sodas and are not suitable in place of a meal. When trying to lose weight, limit your alcohol intake to an occasional beverage. Seek out other types of lower-calorie alcoholic beverages if you enjoy beer and wine, like vodka mixed with soda water, or gin and tonic.

RECIPES

*Makes ten pancakes*
*Nutritional Facts (per one serving size)*
*Calories: 74 | Carbohydrates: 11.5 g | Fat: 1.8 g | Protein: 3 g*

## INGREDIENTS:

- 1 cup of all-purpose flour
- 2 tbsp of toasted wheat germ
- 1/8 tsp of salt
- 1 tsp of baking soda
- 1 cup buttermilk, zero fat
- ¼ cup applesauce, unsweetened
- 2 tsp of vegetable oil of your choice
- 1 large egg
- Optional for garnish: some sliced fresh fruits and/or maple syrup (sugar-free)

## UTENSILS NEEDED:

- 2 medium bowls
- Small bowl (to beat egg)
- ¼ cup scoop
- Non-stick griddle or skillet
- Spatula
- Cooking spray (for skillet or griddle)
- Measuring utensils

## DIRECTIONS:

1. Mix the dry Ingredients: together in a bowl. Combine the buttermilk, applesauce and oil in another bowl. Beat the large egg and add to the wet Ingredients:. Slowly add the wet Ingredients: to the bowl of dry Ingredients:, stirring until everything is just combined. Do not over-stir the batter.

2. Coat the skillet or griddle in the cooking spray and preheat under medium low heat. Add the batter to the skillet in with the scoop, making pancakes about 5" across. Cook until the top of the pancake appears dry, and small bubbles form along the edges. Using the spatula, flip the pancake and cook on the flip side until the pancake is evenly golden brown in appearance.

3. Serve pancakes topped with maple syrup and fresh fruit, or with another type of syrup.

*Makes three 1-cup servings*
*Nutritional Facts (per one serving size)*
*Calories: 122 | Carbohydrates: 31.3 g | Fat: 0.4g | Protein: 1.5g*

### INGREDIENTS:

- 2 cups refrigerated grapefruit sections (about a 24oz jar's worth)
- 1 cup sliced banana (about 1 medium/large banana)
- 1 tbsp freshly chopped mint
- 1 tbsp of honey

### UTENSILS NEEDED:

- Bowl
- Stirring spoon
- Paring knife and cutting board

### DIRECTIONS:

1. Drain the jar of grapefruit pieces but leave about a quarter of the juice in the jar for later use.

2. Combine grapefruit, juice, banana, mint, and honey gently until all the Ingredients: are coated evenly.

3. Serve immediately or, alternatively you can chill for up to 24 hours before serving.

*2 wedges makes for four servings*
*Nutritional Facts (per one serving size)*
*Calories: 184 | Carbohydrates: 10.4 g | Fat: 5.9 g | Protein: 21g*

## INGREDIENTS:

- 1 green bell-pepper
- 8oz pre-sliced mushrooms
- 4 frozen veggie sausage patties
- 1/8 tsp of salt
- 1/8 tsp of pepper
- 1cup of egg substitute like applesauce or mashed banana
- ¼ cup fat free half & half
- ½ cup of sharp cheddar cheese(reduced fat)

## UTENSILS NEEDED:

- Chef's knife
- Microwave
- Oven
- 12" nonstick, oven safe skillet with a lid
- Cooking spray
- Stirring spoon
- Medium bowl
- Cutting board
- Measuring utensils

## DIRECTIONS:

1. Chop the bell pepper. Thaw the patties in the microwave and crumble.

2. Preheat broiler (at the preset broiler temperature).

3. Coat the skillet with cooking spray and heat over medium-high heat. Sauté the bell-pepper and mushrooms in the skillet for about three minutes, or until softened. Add sausage, salt and pepper, and stir until combined. Lower the heat to medium-low and cook for a further one minute.

4. Combine egg substitute and half & half in the medium bowl and pour the mixture over the Ingredients: in the skillet, coating the entire skillet in an even amount. Cover the skillet, and let it cook on medium-low heat for six minutes.

5. Remove the skillet from the heat and sprinkle the dish with the cheddar cheese. Broil in the skillet, in the oven for one to two minutes, until the cheddar cheese has melted. Cut into eight wedges and serve while warm.

*Makes six servings of 1 slice*
*Nutritional Facts:*
*Calories: 138 | Carbohydrates: 8g | Fat: 6g | Protein: 13g*

## INGREDIENTS:

- 2 cups asparagus, sliced into ½ inch chunks
- 1 red bell-pepper
- 1tbsp of water
- 1 cup of low-fat milk
- 2 tbsp of all-purpose flour
- 4 egg whites
- 1Egg WITH yolk

- 1 cup of chopped deli ham (cooked)
- 2 tbsp of fresh basil or tarragon (chopped)
- ½ tsp salt
- ¼ tsp black pepper
- ½ cup of shredded Swiss cheese

## UTENSILS NEEDED:

- Oven
- Microwave safe bowl
- Wax paper
- Microwave
- Colander

- Large mixing bowl
- Whisk
- Stirring spoon
- 9" pie plate
- Cooking spray

## DIRECTIONS:

1. Prepare your Ingredients: (slice the asparagus, chop the bell pepper, separate the four egg whites, chop the deli ham and chop the herbs).

2. Preheat the oven to 350° Fahrenheit.

3. Add the asparagus, bell pepper and water in the microwave safe bowl. Covering the bowl with wax paper, microwave on high for two minutes or until the veggies are slightly tender. Drain them in the colander.

4. Combine the milk and flour in the large bowl using a whisk. Add egg whites and egg and stir until well mixed. Add veggies, ham, tarragon or basil, salt and pepper, and mix well.

5. Coat your pie plate with the cooking spray. Pour in the egg mixture into the pie plate and bake for 35 minutes.

6. Take out quiche and evenly sprinkle the cheese over the top. Bake for a further five minutes or until the center is set and the cheese is melted. Leave to cool slightly before serving. To serve, cut into six wedges.

*Makes twelve servings of 1muffin*
*Nutritional Facts (per one serving size)*
*Calories: 149 | Carbohydrates: 25g | Fat: 4g | Protein: 4g*

## INGREDIENTS:

- ½ cup whole wheat flour
- ¾ cup all-purpose flour
- 2 tsp baking soda
- A pinch of salt
- ¼ tsp ground cinnamon
- ¼ cup brown sugar
- 2 tbsp wheat germ
- ¾ cup raisins
- 1 cup plain, low-fat yogurt
- 3 tbsp canola oil
- 1 egg
- Half an orange

## UTENSILS NEEDED:

- Peel zester
- Oven
- Cupcake cases
- Muffin tin
- Large mixing bowl
- Medium mixing bowl
- Whisk
- Wire cooling rack
- Mixing spoon

## DIRECTIONS:

1. Prepare your Ingredients: (zest the peel of the half an orange, juice your orange half and hold for later).

2. Preheat the oven to 400° Fahrenheit. Set 12 cupcake cases in each of the 12 muffin spots in your tin. Set aside for later use.

3. Add the flour, the baking soda, the salt and the cinnamon to the large mixing bowl. Add the sugar, wheat germ and raisins, and mix to combine. Make a small divet (a hole) in the middle of the dry Ingredients: once mixed.

4. In the medium mixing bowl, use a whisk to blend the yogurt, oil, egg, orange zest and orange juice. Add to the dry Ingredients: by pouring carefully into the divet and then stir to moisten the dry Ingredients:. Do not stir excessively, just combine the Ingredients:.

**5.** Add the mix to the 12 cupcake cases already in the muffin pan, evenly dividing the mixture. Bake for 15-20 minutes, or until you see the muffins have puffed up and have cooked through. Once cool enough to handle, transfer the muffins to the wire cooling rack, and leave to cool. Serve when cool.

*Makes six servings of 4 scones*
*Nutritional Facts:*
*Calories: 152 | Carbohydrates: 27g | Fat: 2g | Protein: 5g*

## INGREDIENTS:

- 1 cup self-rising flour
- 2 tsp sugar
- 1 egg
- 1 tbsp margarine
- ½ cup 1% milk

- Garnishes as desired (blueberries, raspberries, fat-free vanilla yogurt) (about a cup of each)

## UTENSILS NEEDED:

- Cooking spray
- Medium mixing bowl
- Large, nonstick skillet

- Spatula
- Stirring spoon
- Measuring utensils

## DIRECTIONS:

1. Prepare your Ingredients: (beat the egg and melt the margarine).

2. Add the flour and sugar to a medium mixing bowl. Stir to combine. Make a divet in the center of the mixed dry Ingredients:, and pour the egg, margarine and just a little bit of the milk into the divet. Stir slowly and continue to add the remaining milk as you incorporate the liquids into the dry Ingredients:. You should now have a smooth and thick batter.

3. Spray the surface of the skillet with cooking spray. Preheat the skillet over medium to high heat until warm. Drop the scones by the tablespoon onto the hot skillet, creating silver dollar sized pancakes. When they appear dry on the surface and have bubbles along the edge, flip them over and cook on the other side. Once cooked, set on a plate aside and cover, and cook the rest of the batter in this way.

4. Prepare your garnish by gently crushing some of the blueberries and raspberries and serving on the scones with the vanilla yogurt. Serve while the scones are still warm.

*Makes eight servings of 1 popover*
*Nutritional Facts:*
*Calories: 131 | Carbohydrates: 23g | Fat: 2g | Protein: 5g*

## INGREDIENTS:

- 1 cup all-purpose flour
- A pinch of salt
- 1 tsp sugar
- 2 eggs
- 1 cup 1% milk
- ½ cup blueberries
- 1 tbsp powdered sugar (to dust on top)

## UTENSILS NEEDED:

- Cooking spray
- Muffin pan
- Mixing bowl
- Fork
- Whisk
- Wire cooling rack
- Oven
- Measuring utensils

## DIRECTIONS:

1. Preheat the oven to 425° Fahrenheit. Grease eight out of the twelve muffin cups with the cooking spray.

2. Add the flour, salt and sugar to the mixing bowl, and make a divet in the dry Ingredients:. Add the eggs to the well, then adding the milk, beat all of the Ingredients: together with your fork.

3. Little by little, add the flour to the mix and work into the batter with a whisk.

4. Spoon the muffin mix into the tins evenly and drop a few blueberries into each cup. Fill the remaining four cups halfway with water.

5. Placing the tray in the oven, bake for 25-30 minutes or until the popovers have risen and the edges are brown.

6. Remove the popovers with your fork from the tin and serve while warm.

*Makes 1 large loaf with 16 slices*
*Nutritional Facts:*
*Calories: 198 | Carbohydrates: 38g | Fat: 3g | Protein: 7g*

## INGREDIENTS:

- 5 cups of whole wheat flour
- 1 ½ tsp of salt
- 2 tsp of cinnamon
- 1 package instant dry yeast
- 2/3 cup of raisins
- 3 tbsp of sugar
- 3 tbsp of unsalted butter
- 1 cup of skim milk
- 1 egg

## UTENSILS NEEDED:

- 9x5" loaf pan
- Cooking spray
- Small saucepan
- Large mixing bowl
- Stirring spoon
- Surface for kneading (countertop)
- Clean towel
- Wire cooling rack
- Measuring utensils

## DIRECTIONS:

1. Prepare your Ingredients: (beat the egg).

2. Grease the loaf pan with the cooking spray and set aside.

3. Add the flour, salt and cinnamon to a large mixing bowl. Combine with the yeast, raisins and sugar, and make a small divet in the center of the dry Ingredients:.

4. Warm the butter and milk together in the saucepan until the butter has just melted. Carefully add this to the divet in the dry Ingredients:. Add the egg and mix all together, making a dough.

5. Once combined, place the dough on a lightly floured kneading surface like a counter, and knead until smooth and stretchy (for about 10 minutes). Place the dough into the bread pan and cover. Leave the dish covered with the clean towel, for approximately an hour or until it's roughly doubled in size.

6. Preheat the oven to 425° Fahrenheit. Once the bread has risen, remove the towel and place it in the oven. Bake until it has cooked all the way through, which will be around 30 minutes. Remove the bread from the pan after cooking and let it cool on a cooling rack. Serve while warm.

*Makes four servings*
*Nutritional Facts:*
*Calories: 282 | Carbohydrates: 26g | Fat: 13g | Protein: 13g*

## INGREDIENTS:

- 2 tbsp of olive oil
- 1 lb baby portobello or cremini mushrooms
- ½ cup sweet onion (chopped)
- 1 package ready-to-serve brown rice (about 8 oz)
- 1 large carrot
- 1 green onions
- ½ tsp salt
- ¼ tsp pepper
- ¼ tsp pepper
- ¼ tsp caraway seeds
- 4 eggs

## UTENSILS NEEDED:

- Paring knife
- Cutting board
- Large skillet
- Spatula
- Large saucepan
- Slotted spoon

## DIRECTIONS:

1. Prepare your Ingredients: (slice mushrooms, chop onion, grate carrot, thinly slice green onion).

2. Sauté the mushrooms in oil over a medium heat in the large skillet until lightly brown. Add the sweet onion and continue to sauté for one minute. Add the rice and the carrot and cook until the vegetables are tender. Add the green onions, salt, pepper and the caraway seeds and continue cooking until the mix is heated thoroughly.

3. Poach the eggs in the saucepan so the whites are hard, but the yolks have not quite set. Serve the rice mixture with the eggs on top and any extra spices immediately.

*Makes four servings of 1 tostada*
*Nutritional Facts (per one serving size)*
*Calories: 215 | Carbohydrates: 38.7g | Fat: 2.8g | Protein: 13g*

## INGREDIENTS:

- 2 cups of sliced mushrooms
- 2 small zucchinis
- 1 large red bell pepper
- 1 can of reduced sodium refried black beans
- 1 head lettuce
- 1 cup salsa
- ½ cup reduced fat shredded Mexican blend cheese
- 4 tostadas

## UTENSILS NEEDED:

- Chopping knife
- Cutting board
- Medium nonstick skillet
- Stirring spoon
- Measuring utensils

## DIRECTIONS:

1. Prep your veggies (slice mushrooms, slice zucchini, chop bell pepper).

2. Coat the skillet with cooking spray and preheat over medium-high heat. Sauté mushrooms, zucchini and bell peppers until soft (about three to five minutes).

3. Add the Ingredients: to the tostada shells in this order: spoon the refried beans and spread onto the tostada. Spoon the veggie mixture on top of the beans, and add lettuce, salsa and cheese on top to your desired level. Serve while warm.

*Makes six servings of one piece of pizza*
*Nutritional Facts:*
*Calories: 236 | Carbohydrates: 36.2 | Fat: 6.1g | Protein: 10.3g*

## INGREDIENTS:

- ¼ tsp of Italian seasoning
- 1/3 cup of tomato paste
- ¼ cup of water
- 1 prebaked refrigerated pizza crust
- 1 cup shredded part-skim mozzarella
- 1 ½ cups diced bell peppers (2 small green, red and yellow)
- ½ onion

## UTENSILS NEEDED:

- Chopping knife
- Cutting board
- Small mixing bowl
- Oven

## DIRECTIONS:

1. Prepare your Ingredients: (dice the bell peppers and the onion).

2. Preheat the oven to 450° Fahrenheit.

3. Mix the seasoning, the tomato paste and the water in a bowl until well combined. Spread over the pizza crust and top it with the shredded cheese. Add the bell peppers and the onion evenly across the pizza.

4. Bake for ten to twelve minutes or until the cheese has melted. Serve when warm.

*Makes one serving of 1 chicken breast*
*Nutritional Facts:*
*Calories: 262 | Carbohydrates: 8.5g | Fat: 4.1g | Protein: 46.1g*

## INGREDIENTS:

- 1 chicken breast (skinless, boneless)
- 1 oz of low-fat mozzarella
- 1 canned artichoke heart
- 1 tsp of sundried tomato (chopped)
- 5 basil leaves
- 1 clove of garlic
- ¼ tsp curry powder
- ¼ paprika
- 1 pinch pepper

## UTENSILS NEEDED:

- Toothpicks
- Chef's knife
- Cutting board
- Oven
- Baking sheet
- Aluminum foil

## DIRECTIONS:

1. Prepare your Ingredients: (chop up the mozzarella, the artichoke, the basil, the sundried tomato, and the mince garlic clove).

2. Preheat the oven to 365° Fahrenheit.

3. Cut the chicken to almost halfway through with your knife, making a pocket in the chicken. Mix the mozzarella, artichoke, tomato, basil and garlic and stuff into the pocket.

4. Using the toothpicks, close the chicken breast pocket around the stuffing in the center.

5. Put the chicken pocket in the pan and season with the spices mentioned above. Bake for around 20 minutes (or more, depending on the size and thickness of the chicken breast). Remove toothpicks before serving.

SPINACH ROLLS

*Makes two servings*
*Nutritional Facts:*
*Calories: 310 | Carbohydrates: 19.6g | Fat: 10.4g | Protein: 27.3g*

## INGREDIENTS:

- 16 oz of spinach leaves (frozen)
- 3 eggs
- 2 ½ oz of onion
- 2 oz carrots
- 1 oz low-fat mozzarella
- 4 oz fat-free cottage cheese
- ¾ cup of parsley
- 1 clove of garlic
- 1tsp curry powder
- ¼ tsp chili flakes
- 1 tsp salt
- 1 tsp of pepper

## UTENSILS NEEDED:

- Cooking spray
- Microwave
- Oven
- Colander
- Mixing bowl
- Mixing spoon
- Parchment paper
- Baking sheet
- Grater
- Chef's knife
- Cutting board
- Measuring utensils
- Skillet
- Cooking spray

## DIRECTIONS:

1. Prepare your Ingredients: (thaw spinach with the help of a microwave and drain in the colander, finely chop parsley and onion, grate carrots).

2. Preheat the oven to 400° Fahrenheit.

3. Combine the spinach, eggs, mozzarella, garlic, half the salt and the pepper in the mixing bowl.

4. Covering the top of the baking sheet with parchment paper, evenly coat it with cooking spray. Press the mixture of spinach into a mat about 10x12" in size and about a thickness of half an inch on the parchment paper.

5. Bake the mat for 15 minutes. Let cool while preparing the filling.

6. Fry the onions in the skillet with some cooking spray for a little bit. Add the carrots and parsley and simmer for about two minutes. Add the cottage cheese, curry, chili powder, more salt and the pepper and combine momentarily.

31

7. Remove the skillet from the stove, quickly add an egg to the skillet and mix together. Spread the filling over the surface of the spinach mat, leaving a half inch border around the edges of the mat to prevent spillage when rolling.

8. Roll the mat up with care and bake as a roll for another 25 minutes. Let cool before cutting into slices and serving.

*Makes four servings*
*Nutritional Facts:*
*Calories: 336 | Carbohydrates: 10.6g | Fat: 16.8g | Protein: 30.5g*

## INGREDIENTS:

- 1 lbs. beef, cut into strips
- 1 onion, red
- 1 bell-pepper, red
- 1 bell-pepper, yellow
- ½ tsp cumin
- ½tsp of chili powder

- Oil (to cook in)
- Pinch of a salt and pepper to taste
- ½ lime, juiced
- Chopped coriander (fresh)
- 1 avocado

## UTENSILS NEEDED:

- Cast iron skillet
- Chef's knife
- Cutting board

- Measuring utensils
- Metal spatula

## DIRECTIONS:

1. Prepare your Ingredients: (de-seed and slice bell peppers, peel and slice onion, slice avocado, juice lime and chop coriander, slice meat if not pre-sliced).

2. Heat the skillet over a medium heat until nice and hot. Once hot, add the oil and add beef when oil is hot 2-3 strips at a time. Season while in the pan cooking. Sear on each side and then remove from pan and cover on a separate plate. Continue this way until all the strips are cooked.

3. Cook the onion and bell-peppers in the leftover meat juice in the pan. Season with the cumin and the chili powder and stir fry until your desired texture is reached.

4. Serve the meat and veggies with avocado, a little bit of lime juice and a garnish of fresh coriander.

*Makes four servings of 1 pork chop*
*Nutritional Facts:*
*Calories: 405 | Carbohydrates: 16.2g | Fat: 17.1g | Protein: 43.5g*

## INGREDIENTS:

- 4 pork chops
- 1 yellow onion
- 4 cloves of garlic
- 28oz diced tomatoes from a can (i.e. One large can)
- 5 oz low-fat mozzarella
- 1 chicken bouillon cube
- 1 tsp paprika
- 1 tsp of dried oregano
- Salt and pepper to taste

## UTENSILS NEEDED:

- Cooking spray
- Oven
- Chef's knife
- Cutting board
- Frying pan
- Deep sided baking pan

## DIRECTIONS:

1. Prepare your Ingredients: (slice onion into rings, peel and slice garlic, cut fat off pork chops if needed).

2. Preheat the oven to 400 ° Fahrenheit.

3. Spray the frying pan with the cooking spray and sear pork chops on either side, while seasoning with pepper until light brown. Place the chops in the baking pan.

4. Put the onion and the garlic in the frying pan without cleaning and sear the meat juice in. Add the tomato, bouillon and the spices and stir to combine. Let simmer for a minute and pour the mixture over the pork chops in the baking pan.

5. Pour the cheese over the top of the pork chops evenly, and bake for 20 minutes.

6. Let the dish rest for at least 5 minutes before serving.

*Makes four servings*
*Nutritional Facts:*
*Calories: 259 | Carbohydrates: 12g | Fat: 12g | Protein: 26g*

## INGREDIENTS:

- 1 tbsp of canola oil
- 1 lb. of lean ground turkey
- 1 jalapeno pepper
- 2 green onions
- 2 cloves of garlic
- 2 tbsp fresh basil
- 2 tbsp of lime juice
- 2 tbsp of low-sodium soy sauce
- 1-2 tbsp chili garlic sauce (to taste)
- 1 tbsp of sugar or no-calorie sweetener
- 12 large lettuce leaves suitable for lettuce wraps
- 1 medium cucumber
- 1 medium carrot
- 2 cups bean sprouts

## UTENSILS NEEDED:

- Chef's knife
- Paring knife
- Cutting board
- Large skillet
- Spatula
- Spoon

## DIRECTIONS:

1. Prepare your Ingredients: (seed and mince jalapeno, thinly slice green onion, peel and mince garlic, mince basil, julienne cucumber and carrot).

2. Brown turkey in the skillet. Add the jalapeno, the green onions and the garlic and cook until it is aromatic. Add basil, lime juice, soy sauce, chili garlic sauce and sugar and cook until heated thoroughly.

3. Serve in lettuce leaves with cucumber, bean sprouts and carrots. Wrap filling with the leaf.

*Makes four servings of 1 ½ cups*
*Nutritional Facts (per one serving size)*
*Calories: 349 | Carbohydrates: 53.5g | Fat: 12g | Protein: 11.9g*

## INGREDIENTS:

- 1 cup quick-cooking pearl barley
- 1 can of black beans
- 1 pint of grape or cherry tomatoes
- ½ cup chopped green bell pepper
- ½ cup of pepper jack cheese, cut into ¼ inch cubes
- 1/3 cup of lemon juice
- 2 tbsp of olive oil
- 1 tsp of salt
- ¾ cup of fresh cilantro (garnish)
- 1/8 tsp of ground red pepper(garnish)

## UTENSILS NEEDED:

- Chopping knife
- Cutting board
- Microwave safe bowl OR saucepan (for barley, depends on package Directions:)
- Colander
- Medium mixing bowl
- Stirring spoon
- Measuring utensils

## DIRECTIONS:

1. Prep your vegetables and cheese (rinse and drain black beans, halve tomatoes, chop bell pepper, cut cheese into cubes).

2. Cook your barley according to the instructions provided on the package, but do not add any salt. Rinse and, using the colander, drain the barley until it is completely cool.

3. Add black beans, tomatoes, bell pepper, cheese, lemon juice, olive oil and salt to the medium, and mix gently to combine. Add the barley and mix until combined. Serve immediately, garnished with cilantro and red pepper.

*Makes six servings of 1 cup of soup*
*Nutritional Facts:*
*Calories: 98 | Carbohydrates: 12g | Fat: 2g | Protein: 10g*

## INGREDIENTS:

- 1 cup of celery (chopped)
- ½ cup of leeks (thinly sliced, use the white part only)
- ½ cup carrots (chopped)
- ½ cup turnips (chopped)
- 6 cups reduced-sodium, fat free chicken broth
- 1 tbsp minced parsley (fresh)
- 1 ½ tsp fresh thyme (OR ½ tsp of dried thyme)
- 1 tsp of fresh rosemary leaves(minced) (OR ¼ tsp of dried rosemary
- 1 tsp balsamic vinegar
- ¼ tsp of pepper
- 2 oz of uncooked, yolk-free, wide noodles
- 1 cup of chicken breast, cooked and diced

## UTENSILS NEEDED:

- Large saucepan
- Stirring spoon
- Chef's knife
- Cutting board
- Measuring utensils

## DIRECTIONS:

1. Prepare your Ingredients: (chop celery, slice leeks, chop carrots and turnips, mince parsley, mince rosemary, cook and dice chicken breast).

2. Add the celery, leeks, carrots, turnips and 1/3 of a cup of the chicken broth into the saucepan. Cover the pan and cook it on a medium heat for twelve to fifteen minutes or until the veggies are nice and tender. Stir every now and then.

3. Add the remaining chicken broth, the parsley, the thyme, the rosemary, vinegar and pepper to the cooked veggie mix. Bring the whole thing up to boil. Add the noodles in the soup mix and cook until the noodles are done.

4. Now add the chicken to the soup. Lower your heat to a medium level and let it soup simmer until it has heated thoroughly.

*Makes eight servings of ½ of a cup*
*Nutritional Facts:*
*Calories: 62 | Carbohydrates: 9g | Fat: 1g | Protein: 3g*

## INGREDIENTS:

- 1 head of cauliflower (about 2 pounds)
- 1 hard-boiled egg (peeled and chopped)
- ½ cup of red onion (chopped)
- ½ cup of celery(chopped)
- ¼ cup light mayo
- 1 tbsp relish
- 1 tbsp of Dijon mustard
- ¼ tsp celery seed
- ¼ tsp pepper

## UTENSILS NEEDED:

- Chef's knife
- Cutting board
- Measuring utensils
- Medium saucepan
- Colander
- Paper towels
- Large mixing/serving bowl
- Whisk
- Small mixing bowl

## DIRECTIONS:

1. Prepare Ingredients: (peel and chop egg, chop onion, chop celery).

2. Cut off the leaves and core of your cauliflower. Chop florets and stem into bite-sized pieces. You should have roughly four cups of cauliflower pieces after finishing this step.

3. Fill the medium saucepan with water, 2/3rds of the way up and bring it to a boil. Cook the cauliflower in this saucepan until soft but not mushy. Drain and rinse the cauliflower with cold water in a colander to halt the cooking process. Dry the cauliflower using a paper towel to remove any remaining moisture.

4. In the biggest bowl, mix the cauliflower, egg, onion and celery together. In a separate smaller bowl, use a whisk to combine the mayo, relish, mustard, celery seed and pepper. Add the mayo mix to the veggie mix and stir until the cauliflower is thoroughly coated. Chill in the fridge for at least two hours before serving.

*Makes 6 servings of 1 cup of soup*
*Nutritional Facts:*
*Calories: 231 | Carbohydrates: 11.6g | Fat: 12.7g | Protein: 17.1g*

## INGREDIENTS:

- 1 pound of chicken breast
- Salt and pepper as needed
- 1 tbsp coconut oil or vegetable oil
- 1 small onion
- 2 cloves garlic
- 1" piece of ginger
- 1 medium zucchini
- ¾ pound of pumpkin
- 1 red bell pepper
- 1 small chili or jalapeno pepper
- 14oz lite coconut milk
- 2 cups reduced-sodium chicken broth
- 1 lime, juiced
- Cilantro (roughly a handful)

## UTENSILS NEEDED:

- Chef's knife
- Paring knife
- Cutting board
- Measuring utensils
- Large pot (5-6 quarts)
- Stirring spoon

## DIRECTIONS:

1. Prepare your Ingredients: (thinly slice chicken, thinly slice onion into half-moons, mince garlic, peel and mince ginger, cut zucchini into quarters lengthwise and dice, cube pumpkin into 1/2 " thick pieces, remove seeds and slice the red bell pepper thinly, remove seeds and thinly slice the jalapeno, de-stalk cilantro).

2. Add the coconut oil to the pot and put on a high heat. Add the chicken breast and fry until it is no longer pink.

3. Add the onion, the garlic and ginger and keep frying for another 2 to 3 minutes, until a good aroma emerges.

4. Add the zucchini and pumpkin while stirring. Add the bell pepper, jalapeno, coconut milk, chicken broth and lime juice. Combine everything by stirring thoroughly. Bring the soup to a boil, then reduce to a simmer and cover, leaving it to cook for another 20 minutes or until the pumpkin is soft. Season with salt and pepper as desired, and garnish with cilantro.

*Makes eight servings of 1 cup*
*Nutritional Facts:*
*Calories: 253 | Carbohydrates: 9.1g | Fat: 12.3g | Protein: 30.1g*

## INGREDIENTS:

- 1 tbsp of vegetable oil
- 1 yellow onion
- 4 cloves garlic
- 1 tsp cumin
- 1 tsp oregano
- 2 ½ lbs. chicken (cooked and shredded or cubed)
- 16oz salsa verde
- Queso fresco or sour cream (toppings)
- Avocado (diced, topping)
- Fresh coriander (topping)

## UTENSILS NEEDED:

- Chef's knife
- Cutting board
- Measuring utensils
- Large pot
- Stirring spoon

## DIRECTIONS:

1. Prepare your Ingredients: (peel and chop onion and garlic, cook and shred chicken, dice avocado and chop coriander).

2. Add the oil to the pot, and sauté the garlic and onion until aromatic, about 2-3 minutes. Add the cumin and oregano and continue to stir.

3. Add half the salsa verde. Add the chicken breast and the remaining half of the salsa verde. Let sit for 5-7 minutes and allow the flavors to combine.

4. Serve warm. Add avocado, queso fresco / sour cream and coriander as toppings.

*Makes one salad*
*Nutritional Facts:*
*Not available for this recipe*

## INGREDIENTS:

- 1 avocado
- 1 sweet onion, medium sized(Vidalia is preferable)
- 1/3 cup of olive oil
- ¼ cup of stone ground mustard
- 3 tbsp of lemon juice
- 1 tbsp of honey

## UTENSILS NEEDED:

- Chef's knife
- Cutting board
- Small bowl
- Small mixing spoon
- Salad serving bowl

## DIRECTIONS:

1. Prepare your Ingredients: (remove the pit, peel and slice the avocado into thin strips, slice the onion into thin strips).

2. Add the avocado and onion to the serving bowl. In a smaller bowl, mix together the olive oil, mustard, lemon juice and honey. Drizzle the dressing over the avocados and onions in the serving bowl.

3. Stir gently to coat the avocado and onion. Serve immediately alongside a main entrée.

*Makes four servings of a ¾ cup*
*Nutritional Facts (per serving):*
*Calories: 152 | Carbohydrates: 23.8g | Fat: 3.7g | Protein: 6.9g*

## INGREDIENTS:

- 3 cups of unpeeled and cubed Russet potato (roughly one pound of potatoes)
- ½tsp of olive oil
- 1 small onion
- 1 tsp chili powder
- ¼ tsp salt
- ½ cup of shredded reduced-fat sharp cheddar cheese

## UTENSILS NEEDED:

- Chef's knife
- Cutting board
- Steamer basket
- Pot with lid
- Large non-stick skillet

## DIRECTIONS:

1. Prep your Ingredients: (wash and cube potatoes, peel, halve, slice and separate onion into separate rings).

2. Set the potato in a steamer basket over a pot of boiling water. Cover the pot and steam the potatoes for ten minutes, or until they are soft. Remove pot from the heat and drain the potatoes.

3. Preheat the oil in the skillet over a medium-high heat. Add the onion and sauté until tender (about three minutes). Add the potato, the chili powder and salt. Cook Ingredients: for five minutes (until the potato is beginning to brown), making sure to stir frequently. Sprinkle cheese over the potato mixture, cover the skillet, remove from the stove and let it sit until the cheese has melted over the mixture.

4. Serve in serving bowls after the mixture is cool enough to handle.

*Makes 16 servings of single potato cakes*
*Nutritional Facts:*
*Calories: 80 | Carbohydrates: 17g | Fat: 0.8g | Protein: 1.8g*

### INGREDIENTS:

- 2 packages of refrigerated mashed potatoes (roughly 2 ½ pounds)
- 1 tbsp dried onion (minced)
- ½ tsp pepper
- 1 cup matzo meal

### UTENSILS NEEDED:

- Cooking spray
- Large bowl
- Stirring spoon
- Wax paper
- Large, nonstick skillet

### DIRECTIONS:

1. Add the potatoes, dried onion, pepper and matzo meal to the bowl and mix until combined. Divide the potatoes into 16 equal sized portions. Using your hands, pat each potato cake into shape (about four inches in diameter) and place it gently on the wax paper.

2. Preheat the skillet over a medium-high heated stove. Spray each cake with cooking spray. Make sure you spray on both sides and place them in the pan. Lower to a medium heat and cook on either side until brown. Let them cool completely before serving.

*Makes ten servings of 1 slice*
*Nutritional Facts:*
*Calories: 115 | Carbohydrates: 16.4g | Fat: 3.9g | Protein: 3.4g*

## INGREDIENTS:

- 1 ½ cups of all-purpose flour
- 2 tbsp granulated of calorie-free sweetener
- 1 tbsp of baking powder
- 2 tsp ground cumin
- ½ tsp of cumin seed (slightly crushed)
- ¼ tsp of dry mustard
- ¼ tsp of salt
- 2/3 cup of fat-free milk
- 1/3 cup of egg substitute
- 2 ½ tbsp of vegetable oil
- 2 tbsp of picante sauce

## UTENSILS NEEDED:

- Cooking spray
- 2 mixing bowls
- Loaf pan
- Toothpick
- Wire cooling rack

## DIRECTIONS:

1. Preheat the oven to 350° Fahrenheit.

2. Mix the flour, calorie-free sweetener, baking powder, cumin, cumin seed, dry mustard and the salt in a bowl to combine. Make a deep divet in the center of the dry mixture. Mix milk, egg substitute, veggie oil and picante sauce in a separate bowl. Add wet Ingredients: to dry in the divet, mixing until the dry Ingredients: are just moistened.

3. Pour the batter into the loaf pan and bake for 40 minutes, or until the toothpick comes out clean. Remove from the pan and cool on the rack. Serve when cool.

*Makes five servings*
*Nutritional Facts:*
*Calories: 183 | Carbohydrates: 12g | Fat: 2.5g | Protein: 30.7g*

## INGREDIENTS:

- 20oz ground turkey
- 3.5oz fresh spinach (frozen is also okay)
- ¼ cup of oats
- 2 egg whites
- 2 celery stalks
- 3 cloves of garlic
- ½ green bell pepper
- ½ red onion
- ½ cup parsley
- ½ tsp cumin
- 1 tsp mustard powder
- 1 tsp thyme
- ½ tsp turmeric
- ½ tsp chipotle pepper
- 1 tsp salt
- Pepper to taste

## UTENSILS NEEDED:

- Oven
- Food processor
- Large mixing bowl
- Chef's knife
- Cutting board
- Baking sheet
- Parchment paper
- Mixing spoon
- Measuring utensils

## DIRECTIONS:

1. Prepare your Ingredients: (chop the onion, garlic and celery, separate egg whites, chop spinach and the green peppers into dime-sized pieces).

2. Preheat the oven to 350° Fahrenheit.

3. Put the onion, garlic and celery into a food processor and process until it is ground fine. Add to the large mixing bowl. Add the turkey, egg whites and oats, and stir vigorously to combine. Everything should be thoroughly distributed.

4. Add the other veggies to the bowl and continue to mix.

5. Cover your baking sheet with parchment paper and roll your turkey into 15 balls and set them equidistant away from each other, on the baking sheet.

6. Bake the balls for about 25 minutes until cooked all the way through. Let them rest for 5 minutes and serve while warm.

*Makes 3 to 4 servings, depending on the size of your cauliflower*
*Nutritional Facts:*
*Calories: 59 | Carbohydrates: 7.6g | Fat: 2.8g | Protein: 2.8g*

## INGREDIENTS:

- 2 heads cauliflower
- 1 ½ tbsp avocado oil
- ¾ tsp salt

## UTENSILS NEEDED:

- Chef's knife
- Cutting board
- Food processor
- Oven
- Cooking spray
- Baking sheets
- Aluminum foil
- Serving bowl or storage container

## DIRECTIONS:

1. Prepare your Ingredients: (remove the steps and the core from your cauliflower, and chop into 1/2 inch pieces).

2. Preheat the oven to 450° Fahrenheit. Prepare three baking sheets by covering them with aluminum foil and coating with cooking spray. Set aside.

3. Using the food processor, add the cauliflower bit by bit and pulse until the pieces are rice-sized. Continue pulsing until all the cauliflower has been processed. Move the processed cauliflower to a large bowl.

4. Toss the cauliflower with the avocado oil until the cauliflower is evenly coated. Spread the cauliflower evenly across the baking sheets, making sure there are no overlapping pieces.

5. Roast the rice until golden brown, for about 15 minutes. Remove the sheets from your oven and mix. Return the sheets to your oven and cook for another 5 to 6 minutes. Continue this process another time, until the rice is evenly brown.

6. Season your rice with salt and serve immediately, or let cool and store for later use.

*Makes 4 servings*
*Nutritional Information:*
*Not available for this recipe*

## INGREDIENTS:

- 1 cup plum tomatoes
- ½ cup low fat shredded parmesan
- ¼ cup basil, minced
- 3 tbsp of olive oil

- 3 tbsp of parsley, minced
- 3 cloves of garlic, minced
- 2 tbsp of balsamic vinegar
- 1/8 tsp salt
- 1/8 tsp pepper

## UTENSILS NEEDED:

- Mixing bowl and spoon
- Paring knife

- Cutting board

## DIRECTIONS:

1. Prepare your Ingredients: (chop plum tomatoes, mince parsley and basil, peel and mince garlic).

2. Combine all the Ingredients: in a mixing bowl and stir gently to combine, ensuring all the Ingredients: are evenly distributed. Serve immediately on toast points or thick crackers.

*Makes six servings of 1 slice*
*Nutritional Facts (per serving):*
*Calories: 306 | Carbohydrates: 25.6g | Fat: 9.8g | Protein: 27.9g*

## INGREDIENTS:

- 1 pound 97% lean ground chuck
- ½ cup frozen onion, chopped
- 1can Rotel (15oz)
- 1 tsp low sodium taco seasoning
- 1 can refrigerated pizza crust (10oz)

- 1 cup shredded reduced fat sharp cheddar cheese (or skim mozzarella cheese)
- Salsa (topping)
- Reduced fat sour cream (topping)

## UTENSILS NEEDED:

- Large nonstick skillet
- 9x13" cooking pan
- Cooking spray

- Oven
- Pizza cutter or chef's knife

## DIRECTIONS:

1. Preheat oven to 425° Fahrenheit

2. Brown the beef and the onions in the skillet until the beef is nice and crumbly. Drain the mix and return it to the pan. Add the tomatoes and the seasoning, stirring to combine. Cook all over medium high heat for 1 minute (or until warm) and set aside.

3. Spray cooking spray on the baking pan. Remove pizza dough from the can and spread over the bottom of the pan and halfway up the sides. Add the beef mixture all over the dough evenly across the pan.

4. Bake the dough and beef in the oven for twelve minutes. Sprinkle the cheese evenly over the beef, and bake for another five more minutes, or until the cheese melts and the crust is browned along the edges. Let it stand for five to ten minutes before serving, or until the pizza is cool enough to cut and handle. Serve while warm. Top slices with the sour cream and salsa.

*Makes four servings of 1 fillet and ¼ cup of toppings*
*Nutritional Facts:*
*Calories: 215 | Carbohydrates: 5.8g | Fat: 4.9g | Protein: 36.1g*

## INGREDIENTS:

- 2 cups of grape tomatoes
- 2 tbsp capers
- 2 lemons
- 2 tsp of olive oil
- 1 ½ tsp of dried basil(or 1 tbsp of fresh basil)
- ¼ tsp salt
- 1/8tsp of crushed red pepper(optional topping)
- 4 Grouper or snapper filets (6 oz, about ¾ in thick)
- 1 tsp of paprika
- 2 tbsp of chopped parsley(fresh)

## UTENSILS NEEDED:

- Cooking spray
- Mixing bowl
- Mixing spoon
- Broiler pan
- Aluminum foil
- Cooking spray

## DIRECTIONS:

1. Prep your Ingredients: (halve the tomatoes, drain the capers, squeeze one lemon's worth of juice and cut the other lemon into four wedges, chop the basil if using fresh and chop the parsley).

2. Preheat the oven at 450 ° Fahrenheit.

3. Mix the tomatoes, capers, lemons, olive oil, basil, salt, and crushed red pepper in a bowl. Set aside for later.

4. Cover your broiler pan with aluminum foil, on one side and spray with cooking spray. Place the fish on the aluminum foil. Sprinkle the paprika evenly over your fish, and then spray your fish with cooking spray. Bake for about 10 minutes.

5. Top the fish with the veggie mix and cook for a further 5 minutes. Garnish with fresh parsley and a lemon wedge. Serve while warm.

*Makes four servings of ¾ cup scallops and 1 cup of pasta*
*Nutritional Facts:*
*Calories: 375 | Carbohydrates: 36.9g | Fat: 9.7g | Protein: 34.8g*

## INGREDIENTS:

- 8 oz of uncooked spinach fettuccine
- 1 ½ lbs. scallops
- ¾ tsp of pepper
- 2 tbsp of olive oil
- 1 tbsp of Dijon mustard
- 1 tbsp of chopped basil(fresh)
- ¼ tsp of salt
- ¾ of dry white wine or low-sodium chicken broth
- 2green onions
- 3 tbsp of chopped parsley(fresh)

## UTENSILS NEEDED:

- Cooking spray
- Boiling pot
- Colander
- Large nonstick skillet
- spatula
- Cooking spray
- Mixing bowl

## DIRECTIONS:

1. Prep your Ingredients: (chop the basil, green onions and parsley).

2. Cook the pasta according to the package Directions:. Don't add any salt or fat. Drain the pasta in a colander.

3. Rinse the scallops and pat dry. Sprinkle pepper over the scallops. Coat your pan with the cooking spray, and heat over a stove on medium high heat until warm. Cook half of the scallops on both sides three minutes each (or until done). Repeat for the second half.

4. In another bowl, add olive oil, Dijon mustard, chopped basil and salt and mix to combine. Set aside.

5. Reheat the first skillet on the stove. Add the wine and the green onions and cook for one minute. Add your olive oil mixture and cook briefly then add the scallops and cook briefly again while stirring continuously. Serve the pasta topped with the scallops and sauce and garnish with the fresh chopped parsley.

*Makes five servings of 1 kebab*
*Nutritional Facts:*
*Calories: 172 | Carbohydrates: 7.4g | Fat: 7.1g | Protein: 21.2g*

## INGREDIENTS:

- 1 lb. of beef tenderloin
- 2 tsp of Worcestershire sauce
- 1 medium sized green bell pepper
- 10 tomatoes (cherry)
- 10 mushrooms (small)
- 2 yellow squash (small)
- 1/8 tsp of black pepper
- ¼ tsp of salt

## UTENSILS NEEDED:

- Cooking spray
- Grill
- Metal skewers (12" in length)

## DIRECTIONS:

1. Prep your Ingredients: (chop the bell pepper into 20 squares, cut the squash into 10 slices.

2. Prepare the grill for usage by coating the grill rack with cooking spray.

3. Cut the tenderloin into 20 cubes. Douse the meat in Worcestershire sauce. Stick the meat, bell-pepper, cherry tomatoes, mushrooms and squash onto five skewers, alternating them. Sprinkle some black pepper over the skewers.

4. Grill the skewers uncovered on the rack for about 10 minutes (or until you are satisfied with their doneness). Sprinkle skewers with salt.

*Makes four servings of 1 chicken breast and ¼ cup avocado mixture*
*Nutritional Information:*
*Calories: 221 | Carbohydrates: 5.2g | Fat: 10.3g | Protein: 27.4g*

## INGREDIENTS:

- 1 ½ tsp of blackened seasoning
- 4 skinless, boneless chicken breast halves (about 4oz each)
- 1 tsp olive oil
- 1 avocado
- 2 tbsp chopped cilantro (fresh)
- 1 jalapeno pepper
- 2 limes
- ¼ tsp salt

## UTENSILS NEEDED:

- Large nonstick skillet
- Spatula
- Mixing bowl
- Mixing spoon

## DIRECTIONS:

1. Prepare your Ingredients: (peel and slice the avocado, de-seed and finely chop jalapeno, juice one lime and slice the other into fourths).

2. Season the chicken on both sides with the blackening seasoning. Preheat the oil in the skillet on high heat. Add the seasoned chicken to the pan, and sear briefly on one side. Reduce the heat to medium and cook the chicken on both sides until browned (should be about three minutes).

3. Combine the remaining Ingredients: in a bowl. Serve chicken with avocado mixture on top, and with a fourth of a lime squeezed onto each piece.

*Makes four servings of one slice*
*Nutritional Facts:*
*Calories: 220 | Carbohydrates: 13g | Fat: 7g | Protein: 26g*

## INGREDIENTS:

- ¾ reduced sodium tomato sauce
- 2 egg whites
- 4 tbsp of reduced-sodium chunky salsa
- ½ tsp pepper
- ½ cup steel cut oats

- ½ onion (minced)
- 1/3 canned mushroom stems and pieces (drained, chopped)
- 1 of clove garlic(minced)
- 8oz lean ground turkey
- 8oz of 96% lean ground beef

## UTENSILS NEEDED:

- Chef's knife
- Cutting board
- Aluminum foil
- Oven
- Cooking spray

- Measuring utensils
- Medium mixing bowl
- Large mixing bowl
- Stirring spoon
- Broiler pan

## DIRECTIONS:

1. Prep your Ingredients: (mince onion, drain and chop mushroom stems and pieces, mince garlic,).

2. Preheat oven to 350° Fahrenheit. Cover the broiler pan with some aluminum foil and coat with cooking spray. Set aside for later.

3. Combine ½ a cup of tomato sauce, the egg whites, 3 tbsp of the salsa, and the pepper in the medium bowl. Add the oatmeal, the onion, the mushrooms and the garlic. Combine thoroughly.

4. Add the turkey and beef to the large bowl and stir to combine. Add the tomato mixture and mix until completely incorporated.

5. Move the meat over to the broiler pan and shape into a 4x8" loaf. Combine the salsa and the remaining tomato sauce in a smaller bowl and pour over the top of the loaf.

6. Bake the whole thing for 55 minutes, or until cooked thoroughly with the inside temperature reaching 165 ° Fahrenheit. Let stand for at least five minutes before handling. Serve while warm.

*Makes four servings of 4oz of meat*
*Nutritional Facts (per serving):*
*Calories: 268 | Carbohydrates: 4.6g | Fat: 13.5g | Protein: 25.6g*

## INGREDIENTS:

- 16oz turkey breast
- ¼ cup of olive oil
- 1/3 cup of balsamic vinegar
- 1 tsp of garlic powder
- 1 tsp of dried basil
- 1 tsp of thyme
- 1 tsp of pepper

## UTENSILS NEEDED:

- Large Ziploc bag
- Chef's knife
- Cutting board
- Skillet

## DIRECTIONS:

1. Combine all Ingredients: except the turkey in the Ziploc bag. Seal the Ziploc bag and shake vigorously to combine.

2. Cut the turkey breast into strips no thicker than an inch and soak in the Ziploc bag with the marinade for a minimum of a half an hour.

3. Fry the meat in a skillet under medium heat until fully cooked (about 5-8 minutes). Serve with rice or quinoa, and mixed vegetables or a fresh salad.

*Makes one serve of one chicken breast*
*Nutritional Facts:*
*Calories: 294 | Carbohydrates: 2.4g | Fat: 11.5g | Protein: 38.6g*

## INGREDIENTS:

- 1 chicken breast
- 1 ½ oz finely sliced prosciutto
- 1 ¼oz of low-fat cream cheese
- 5-10 of basil leaves
- Salt and pepper

## UTENSILS NEEDED:

- Aluminum foil
- Baking sheet
- Butter knife

## DIRECTIONS:

1. Preheat the oven at 380 ° Fahrenheit.

2. Lay out the prosciutto on the aluminum foil so the edges overlap a little bit. Spread the cream cheese evenly across the prosciutto. Lay the basil on top so they totally cover the cream cheese.

3. Take the chicken breast and wrap the prosciutto layers around the chicken. Garnish with a little bit of salt and pepper.

4. Bake the chicken for 25-30 minutes, or until fully cooked.

5. Let the chicken rest for one minute before serving. Serve while warm with a side.

*Makes six servings*
*Nutritional Facts:*
*Calories: 113 | Carbohydrates: 9g | Fat: 5g | Protein: 9g*

## INGREDIENTS:

- 1 medium onion
- 1 tbsp of butter
- 3 medium zucchinis
- 3 medium tomatoes
- 1 cup of shredded reduced-fat Swiss cheese
- 1/3 cup of reduced-fat sour cream
- 1 tsp of paprika
- ½ tsp of salt
- ½ tsp of garlic powder
- ¼ tsp of pepper
- 2 tbsp of shredded Parmesan

## UTENSILS NEEDED:

- Chef's knife
- Cutting board
- Large nonstick skillet
- Large mixing bowl
- 11x7" baking dish
- Cooking spray

## DIRECTIONS:

1. Prepare your Ingredients: (chop the onion, shred and pat the zucchini dry, seed and chop up the tomatoes).

2. Preheat the oven to 350° Fahrenheit. Coat the baking dish with the cooking spray and set it aside.

3. Sauté the onions in butter in the large skillet until lightly brown. Put onions, zucchini, tomatoes, half the swiss cheese, sour cream and seasonings into the mixing bowl and stir to combine thoroughly.

4. Transfer the mix to the baking pan, sprinkle it with the rest of the cheeses, and bake for 25-30 minutes. Let it cool for 10 minutes and serve while warm.

*Makes four servings*
*Nutritional Facts:*
*Calories: 203 | Carbohydrates: 3g | Fat: 9g | Protein: 27g*

## INGREDIENTS:

- 1 ½ tsp olive oil
- 1 ¾ sliced fresh mushrooms
- 3 sliced green onions
- 3 cups of fresh spinach
- 2 tbsp pecans (chopped)
- 4 chicken breast halves approximately 4oz each
- ½ tsp of rotisserie chicken seasoning
- 2 slices of low-fat provolone cheese

## UTENSILS NEEDED:

- Chef's knife
- Cutting board
- Large skillet
- Spatula
- Broiler pan
- Cooking spray

## DIRECTIONS:

1. Prepare your Ingredients: (slice the mushrooms, slice the green onions, chop the pecans, halve the chicken breasts and the provolone slices).

2. Preheat the broiler.

3. Sauté the mushrooms and green onions over medium-high heat in the skillet until tender. Add the spinach and pecans. Remove from the heat but do keep it warm.

4. Season chicken with rotisserie seasoning and grill in the broiler pan until cooked thoroughly. Flip if needed. Top it off with cheese and broil until it has melted.

5. Let chicken sit for at least 5 minutes and serve with mushroom-spinach mix while warm.

*Makes four servings of 3 tablespoons (3/4 cup total)*
*Nutritional Facts (per serving, not including veggies or chips)*
*Calories: 64 | Carbohydrates: 4g | Fat: 5g | Protein: 2g*

## INGREDIENTS:

- 1 avocado, ripe
- 1 tbsp lime juice
- ¼ cup nonfat Greek yogurt, plain
- 1 tsp Dijon mustard
- ¼ tsp salt
- Fresh chives (optional garnish)

## UTENSILS NEEDED:

- Fork or potato masher
- Shallow bowl

## DIRECTIONS:

1. Prepare your Ingredients: (peel and pit the avocado, chop the chives).

2. With a fork, mash the avocado in the bowl until creamy (you can also leave some chunks if desired). Add in the rest of the Ingredients: and mix until combined. Serve immediately with some pita chips or raw veggies or chill up to 6 hours before serving.

*Makes twelve servings of 1 snack cup*
*Nutritional Facts:*
*Calories: 72 | Carbohydrates: 12g | Fat: 2g | Protein: 2g*

## INGREDIENTS:

- 1 ¼ cups 2% milk
- ½ cup of egg substitute
- 1/3 cup of sugar
- 1 tsp of vanilla
- 1/8 tsp of salt
- 1/8 tsp nutmeg
- 4 cups cinnamon raisin bread cut into cubes (about 6 slices cut into ½" cubes)
- 1 tbsp margarine, melted

## UTENSILS NEEDED:

- Bread knife
- Cutting board
- Muffin tray
- Cupcake liners
- Medium sized mixing bowl
- Stirring spoon
- Wire cooling rack

## DIRECTIONS:

1. Prepare your Ingredients: (cut your bread into cubes and melt the margarine).

2. Preheat the oven to 350 ° Fahrenheit. Line the muffin pan with 12 cupcake liners.

3. Add the milk, the egg substitute, the sugar, the vanilla, salt and nutmeg to the medium sized bowl and mix until combined. Add the bread cubes and mix until all the bread has been completely coated in liquid. Let the bowl sit in a room temperature environment for around 15 minutes.

4. Add the bread mix evenly to the 12 cupcake liners in the pan. Spoon the margarine evenly over the twelve cups.

5. Bake the muffins for 30 mins, or until they are golden brown on the top and nice and puffy. Place them on the wire cooling rack and let cool completely before serving.

*Makes four servings of one smoothie*
*Nutritional Facts:*
*Calories: 108 | Carbohydrates: 21g | Fat: 2g | Protein: 4g*

## INGREDIENTS:

- ♦ 4 cups strawberries
- ♦ 1 cup plain, low-fat yogurt
- ♦ ½ cup orange juice
- ♦ 1 tbsp sugar
- ♦ 4 strawberries and 4 slices orange (for garnish, optional)

## UTENSILS NEEDED:

- ♦ Food processor or blender
- ♦ Colander
- ♦ Silicone spatula

## DIRECTIONS:

1. Rinse the strawberries in the colander and drain of any excess liquid. Place them in the blender with the yogurt, orange juice and sugar. Blend them on the highest setting until well-blended and a smoothie-like texture appears. Scrape the sides with the silicone spatula to remove any dry or unblended Ingredients:, and pulse to blend into the mixture.

2. Pour smoothie into four tall glasses and serve immediately

*Makes sixteen servings of ¼ cup*
*Nutritional Facts:*
*Not available for this recipe*

## INGREDIENTS:

- ◆ 1 cup roasted peanuts
- ◆ 1 cup raw or roasted almonds
- ◆ 1 cup pumpkin seeds
- ◆ 2 oz dark chocolate chips
- ◆ ½ raisins or craisins

## UTENSILS NEEDED:

- ◆ Large Ziploc bag

## DIRECTIONS:

1. Combine all the Ingredients: in a large Ziploc bag. Shake to combine thoroughly. Serve immediately or keep in Ziploc bag for later serving.

## Tips:

Other variations on this recipe can include different sources of protein and flavor. Some popular additions or substitutions to the Ingredients: listed above are dried pineapple, sesame sticks, roasted pecans, popcorn, banana chips and miniature pretzels. Feel free to adjust this recipe to your taste.

*Makes four servings of 2/3 cup berries and ¼ cup maple cream*
*Nutritional Facts (per one serving size)*
*Calories: 140 | Carbohydrates: 31.4g | Fat: 0.4g | Protein: 2.2g*

## INGREDIENTS:

- ¾ cup fat-free sour cream
- ¼ cup maple syrup
- 1 cup blueberries
- 1 ½ cup raspberries

## UTENSILS NEEDED:

- Small mixing bowl
- Whisk
- Serving spoon
- Colander
- Dessert dishes

## DIRECTIONS:

1. Mix sour cream and maple syrup together in the bowl, and whisk until thoroughly combined.

2. Rinse berries in a colander.

3. Combine berries in your serving dessert dishes. Pour maple cream over the berries. Serve immediately or chill up to 24 hours before serving.

*Makes nine servings of 1 square*
*Nutritional Facts (per one serving size)*
*Calories: 232 | Carbohydrates: 34.2g | Fat: 10.1g | Protein: 6.3g*

## INGREDIENTS:

- 1 package sugar-free chocolate cookie sandwiches (like Oreo's)
- 1/3 cup pecans, chopped
- 3 tbsp reduced-calorie margarine
- 1 qt vanilla sugar free, fat free ice cream

## UTENSILS NEEDED:

- Chopping knife
- Cutting board
- Ziploc baggie
- Medium mixing bowl
- Stirring spoon
- Measuring utensils
- 9" pan
- Plastic wrap

## DIRECTIONS:

1. Prep your Ingredients: (crush the cookies in a Ziploc bag, chop pecans, melt margarine, soften ice cream).

2. Combine the cookies, pecans and margarine and set one cup of your mixture aside. Press the rest into the bottom of the 9" pan. Place it in the freezer for ten minutes.

3. Spread your ice cream over the top of the crust. Sprinkle the remaining crust mixture over the top of the ice cream, and press gently into the ice cream. Cover the whole pan with some plastic wrap and freeze for at least eight hours before serving. Let stand for five minutes and cut into nine squares for serving.

*Makes five servings of 1 cup*
*Nutritional Facts (per one serving size)*
*Calories: 93 | Carbohydrates: 18.9g | Fat: 0.5g | Protein: 5.1g*

## INGREDIENTS:

- 1 large cantaloupe
- 1/3 cup calorie-free granulated sweetener
- 2 tbsp lemon juice
- 2 tsp unflavored Jell-O
- ¼ cold water
- 1 8oz carton fat-free sugar-free vanilla yogurt
- Cantaloupe wedge (garnish)

## UTENSILS NEEDED:

- Chopping knife
- Cutting board
- Blender (or food processor)
- Large mixing bowl
- Small saucepan
- Stirring spoon
- 8" square pan
- Counter or hand mixer
- Measuring utensils

## DIRECTIONS:

1. Prep your Ingredients: (peel and chop the cantaloupe, set aside a wedge for garnish).

2. Add the cantaloupe, the sweetener and lemon juice into a blender. Blend until the mixture is smooth. Pour mixture into the bowl.

3. Pour Jell-O mix into cold water in the small saucepan. Stir to combine. Let the mixture stand for 1 minute, then cook over low heat, stirring all the time until the Jell-O dissolves (about four minutes). Now add this to the cantaloupe mixture and mix thoroughly. Next, add the yogurt, and stir mixture until thoroughly combined and smooth.

4. Pour the entire mixture into the square pan and freeze until almost firm.

5. Move the mix back into the mixing bowl used previously and beat it with a mixer until fluffy at a high speed.

6. Return the beat mixture into the pan and freeze until completely firm.

7. Serve by scooping into individual dishes. Garnish each dish with a cantaloupe wedge.

*Makes twenty servings of 1 sandwich cookie*
*Nutritional Facts:*
*Calories: 97 | Carbohydrates: 13.3g | Fat: 4.3g | Protein: 2.5g*

## INGREDIENTS:

- ¼ cup of margarine
- ¼ cup of natural creamy peanut butter
- ½ cup of granulated calorie-free sweetener
- ¼ cup of sugar
- 2 large egg whites
- 1 tsp of vanilla extract
- 1 ¾ of all-purpose flour
- 1 tsp of baking soda
- 1/8 of tsp salt
- ¾ cup of low-sugar jam

## UTENSILS NEEDED:

- Cooking spray
- Hand mixer
- Baking sheets
- Flat bottomed glass
- Wire rack

## DIRECTIONS:

1. Prep your Ingredients: (soften margarine, separate out egg whites).

2. Preheat oven to 350 ° Fahrenheit.

3. Beat together margarine and peanut butter until creamy at a medium pace. Add the sweetener and sugar little by little. Add the egg whites and vanilla while continuing to beat. In a separate bowl, mix in the flour, baking soda and salt together. Gradually add this mix to the creamy mixture, all while beating.

4. Form 40 one inch balls with the dough and flatten with the glass once on the baking sheet. Bake for eight minutes or until brown on the edges. Cool on a wire rack.

5. Spread 1 ½ tsp of the jam onto the bottom of 20 cookies and top with the other cookies.

*Makes six servings of ¾ of a cup*
*Nutritional Facts:*
*Calories: 148 | Carbohydrates: 14g | Fat: 9g | Protein: 4g*

## INGREDIENTS:

- 3 tbsp butter
- 2 tbsp all-purpose flour
- ¾ cup no-sugar added apricot jam or preserves
- ¼ warm water
- 1/3 cup dried apricots (chopped finely)
- 3 beaten egg yolks
- 4 egg whites
- ¼ tsp cream of tartar
- 1/8 tsp of salt

## UTENSILS NEEDED:

- Oven
- Chef's knife
- Cutting board
- Measuring utensils
- Medium saucepan
- Stirring spoon
- Whisk
- Small mixing bowl
- Hand electric mixer
- ½ quart souffle dish

## DIRECTIONS:

1. Prepare your Ingredients: (separate eggs and beat yolks, chop apricots finely).

2. Preheat the oven to 325 ° Fahrenheit. Melt butter in the saucepan and add flour. Stir together until mixture gets bubbly. Add the fruit spread, water and apricots. Cook in the saucepan while stirring until thickened (or about three minutes). Remove saucepan from the stove, and using a whisk, whisk in the egg yolks. Let the mixture cool to room temperature, whilst stirring once in a while.

3. Beat your egg whites, cream of tartar and the salt together in the smaller bowl, preferably with an electric hand mixer at a high speed, until you can see stiff peaks forming in the mix. Fold with care into the apricot mix. Pour into the soufflé dish and bake for 30 mins until puffy and golden brown. Serve while warm.

*Makes one cake*
*Nutritional Information:*
*Not available for this recipe*

## INGREDIENTS:

- 1 package chocolate cake mix
- 1 package sugar free instant chocolate pudding mix
- 1 ¾ water

- 3 egg whites
- Low-fat whipped cream and strawberries (garnish)

## UTENSILS NEEDED:

- Mixing spoon
- Mixing bowl
- Electric mixer

- 8" round cake pan
- Cooking spray

## DIRECTIONS:

1. Preheat your oven to 350 ° Fahrenheit. Grease your cake pan on the inside with cooking spray and set aside.

2. Prepare your Ingredients: (separate your egg whites).

3. Combine the cake mix, pudding mix, water and egg whites in the mixing bowl. Beat at a low speed for 1 minutes (until Ingredients: are combined) and on a medium speed for another two minutes.

4. Pour the mix into your prepared cake pan and bake until cooked through (you should be able to stick and remove a toothpick into the center and have it come out clean), or for about 35-40 minutes. Serve warm with the whipped cream and strawberries.

# DAY I

## Breakfast

## *2 HARDBOILED EGGS*

*Calories: 156*
*Carbohydrates: 0% (1.2g) | Fat: 15% (10g) | Protein: 24% (12g)*

**INGREDIENTS:**

- ◆ 6 – 12 eggs
- ◆ Salt
- ◆ Pepper

**DIRECTIONS:**

1. Prepare a large pot with boiling hot water.
2. Set 6-12 eggs in the boiling water and reduce the heat to a simmer
3. Cook for about 10 minutes
4. Drain water, and peel eggs in cold water
5. Season with salt and pepper
6. These can be prepped beforehand and used as a quick breakfast or an on-the-go snack.

Lunch: Veggie Tostadas (See page 28)

Dinner: Prosciutto Wrapped Chicken Breast (See page 61)

# DAY 2

Breakfast: Applesauce Pancakes (See page 15)

Lunch:

## PITA WITH HAVARTI CHEESE AND SMOKED TURKEY

*Calories: 389*
*Carbohydrates: 86% (27.65g) | Fat: 89% (17.95g) | Protein: 74% (28.69g)*

### INGREDIENTS:

- 1 Pita Bread
- 1 slice of Havarti cheese
- 3 oz Smoked Turkey
- Thinly sliced Granny apple (optional)

### DIRECTIONS:

1. Make yourself a delicious sandwich

Dinner: Deep Dish Taco Pizza (See page 53)

# DAY 3

Breakfast : Mushroom and Brown Rice Hash
with poached Eggs (See page 26)

Lunch : Onion and Avocado Salad (See page 80)

Dinner:

## TOMATO SOUP AND KALE/APPLE SALAD

*Calories: 417*
*Carbohydrates: 23% (56g)| Fat: 41% (20g)| Protein: 28% (15.23g)*

### INGREDIENTS:

- 1 cup tinned tomato soup
- 5 oz baby kale leaves
- 1 large apple
- ¼ cup sunflower seeds
- Vinaigrette of your choice.

### DIRECTIONS:

1. Prepare soup as directed on the tin
2. Add all the salad Ingredients: together

# DAY 4

Breakfast:

## *OATMEAL*

*Calories: 116*
*Carbohydrates: 13% (31.12g) | Fat: 7% (3.3g) | Protein: 15% (8.13g)*

**INGREDIENTS:**

- ◆ ½ cup steel cut oats
- ◆ Toppings of your choice.

**DIRECTIONS:**

1. Heat a cup of water in a medium-sized saucepan
2. Bring to the boil
3. Add the oats, return to a boil
4. Lower the heat and cover for 2 – 3 mins, or until desired thickness
5. Add your choice of toppings (which could be anything from peanut butter, chia seeds, berries, etc)

Lunch: Three-Pepper Pizza (See page 29)

Dinner: Snapper with Tomato Caper topping (See page 54)

# DAY 5

Breakfast : Honey Grapefruit with Banana (See page 16)

Lunch:

## *FANCY GRILLED CHEESE*

*Calories: 220*
*Carbohydrates: 8% (20.14g) | Fat: 22% (10.8g) | Protein: 19% (10.27g)*

### INGREDIENTS:

- ◆ 2 slices wholegrain bread
- ◆ 1 slice cheddar cheese
- ◆ Toppings of your choice.

### DIRECTIONS:

1. Grill the slices of wholegrain bread in a cooking-spray coated pan, until toasty on one side.
2. Add the cheese and your choice of toppings.
3. Combine the slices so the cheese is facing down and cook until golden on both sides, and the cheese is melted.

Dinner: Basil Scallops with Spinach fettucine (See page 55)

# DAY 6

Breakfast: Cinnamon Raisin Bread (See page 24)

Lunch: Coconut Chicken Soup (See page 40)

Dinner:

## *"GREEK" WRAP*

*Calories: 532*
*Carbohydrates: 18% (45.04g) | Fat: 58% (28.39g) | Protein: 47% (25.48g)*

**INGREDIENTS:**

- 1 whole wheat tortilla
- 2 slices turkey meat
- 1/3 cup hummus
- Chopped tomato
- ½ cup feta cheese
- Some black olives
- 1 cup spinach

**DIRECTIONS:**

1. Wrap everything into the whole wheat tortilla for a quick and filling dinner

# DAY 7

Breakfast:

## *MUESLI*

*Calories: 220*
*Carbohydrates: 15% (36.66g) | Fat: 13% (6.2g) | Protein: 14% (7.53g)*

### INGREDIENTS:

- ½ cup muesli
- ½ cup 2% milk (or almond milk)
- Toppings of your choice

### DIRECTIONS:

1. Combine the muesli with the milk and add any toppings of your choice. Could be low-fat yoghurt, strawberries, bananas, etc.

Lunch: Healthy Stuffed Chicken Breast (See page 30)

Dinner: Beef Kebabs (See page 56)

# DAY 8

Breakfast: Veggie Sausage Fritatta (See page 17)

Lunch:

## MASON JAR SALAD

*Nutritional info will differ every time*

........................................................................................................

**INGREDIENTS:**

- ♦ Gather any of your favorite salad Ingredients:

**DIRECTIONS:**

Add Ingredients: in this order:
1. Salad dressing
2. Proteins like cheese or meat
3. Fatty veggies or legumes
4. Other veggies
5. Leafy greens
6. One idea: Avo, Corn, Black Beans, Chunky Salsa, Cilantro, Mixed Greens

Dinner: Seared Chicken with Avocado (See page 57)

# DAY 9

Breakfast: Blueberry Popovers (See page 23)

Lunch: Low Carb Cauliflower "Potato" Salad (See page 39)

Dinner:

## *BURRITO BOWL*

*Calories: 314*
*Carbohydrates: 15% (36.99) | Fat: 39% (18.85g) | Protein: 17% (9.05g)*

**INGREDIENTS:**

- 15oz black beans
- Handful leafy greens
- Your choice of fajita grilled veggies
- Guacamole
- Salsa
- Green chilies (optional)

**DIRECTIONS:**

1. Instead of the traditional rice, use a base of beans and leafy greens. Top with fajita grilled veggies of your choice, and some store-bought (or homemade) guacamole, salsa and chilies.

# DAY 10

Breakfast:

## *WHOLEGRAIN ENGLISH MUFFIN*

*Calories: 127*
*Carbohydrates: 10% (25.54g) | Fat: 2% (1.14g) | Protein: 9% (4.96g)*

**INGREDIENTS:**

- ◆ 1 Wholegrain English Muffin
- ◆ Spreads of your choice

**DIRECTIONS:**

2. Slice the muffin in half and toast lightly. Top with a spread of your choice, such as low-fat ricotta, avocado, or sunflower butter

Lunch: Spinach Rolls (See page 31)

Dinner: Authentic Meatloaf (See page 58)

# DAY 11

Breakfast: Crustless Ham and Aparagus Quiche (See page 18)

Lunch:

## BBQ CHICKEN WRAP

*Calories: 539*
*Carbohydrates: 26% (63.51g) | Fat: 26% (12.65g) | Protein: 80% (43.86g)*

### INGREDIENTS:

- 1 Wholegrain Tortilla Wrap
- 1 cups shredded cooked chicken
- ¼ cup BBQ sauce
- Shredded Carrots
- Strips of bell peppers
- Chopped red onion

### DIRECTIONS:

1. Spread the BBQ sauce over the tortilla. Add the carrots, bell peppers, onions and chicken and wrap together.

Dinner: Marinated Turkey Breast (See page 60)

# DAY 12

Breakfast: Drop Scones (See page 22)

Lunch : Veggie Chicken Noodle Soup (See page 38)

Dinner:

## TUNA SALAD

*Calories: 394*
*Carbohydrates: 2% (5.74g) | Fat: 35% (17g) | Protein: 100% (54.85g)*

## INGREDIENTS:

- ◆ 1 tin tuna
- ◆ 3 tablespoons mayonnaise
- ◆ 2 tablespoons Greek yoghurt
- ◆ Chopped celery
- ◆ 1 teaspoon lemon juice
- ◆ Handful leafy greens

## DIRECTIONS:

1. Drain your tuna from the liquid in the tin. Add all Ingredients: together over a bed of leafy greens.

# DAY 13

## Breakfast:

### LOW-FAT UNSWEETENED GREEK YOGHURT AND FRUITS

*Calories: 148*
*Carbohydrates: 4% (9g) | Fat: 2% (0.98g) | Protein: 47% (25.48g)*

### INGREDIENTS:

- ◆ 1 cup Low-fat unsweetened Greek Yoghurt
- ◆ Fruits of your choice for toppings

### DIRECTIONS:

1. Pour into a bowl and add your choice of toppings.

## Lunch: Beef Fajitas (See page 33)

## Dinner: Prosciutto Wrapped Chicken Breast (See page 61)

# DAY 14

Breakfast: Breakfast Muffins (See page 20)

Lunch:

## *EGGS FOR LUNCH*

*Calories:429*
*Carbohydrates: 12% (29.3g) | Fat: 46% (22.24g) | Protein: 51% (27.78g)*

### INGREDIENTS:

- ◆ 2 eggs
- ◆ 1/8 cup of milk
- ◆ 1 wholegrain English muffin
- ◆ Slice of ham
- ◆ Slice of Clementine (optional)

### DIRECTIONS:

1. Add your eggs and milk together and whisk thoroughly
2. Heat the butter in a non-stick pan until melted
3. Pour in the egg mixture
4. As the eggs begin to set, gently pull together using a spatula forming little balls
5. Continue cooking, stirring occasionally, until all liquid has gone
6. Serve on the muffin with ham and Clementine

Dinner: Zucchini Tomato Bake (See page 62)

# DAY 15

Breakfast: Applesauce Pancakes (See page 15)

Lunch: Barley and Black Bean Salad (See page 37)

Dinner:

## CHARCUTERIE DINNER

*Calories: 709*
*Carbohydrates: 27% (65.67g) | Fat: 83% (40.27g) | Protein: 47% (25.88g)*

**INGREDIENTS:**

- ◆ 1 hardboiled egg
- ◆ Some seed crackers
- ◆ A stick of low-fat string cheese
- ◆ Sliced apple
- ◆ Sliced celery
- ◆ A few carrot sticks
- ◆ Some nut butter

**DIRECTIONS:**

1. Serve all Ingredients: on a cheeseboard, charcuterie style. Pair different toppings on the crackers.

# DAY 16

Breakfast:

## *OMELET*

*Calories: 88g*
*Carbohydrates: 0% (0.63g) | Fat: 17% (8.37g) | Protein: 20% (11.05g)*

**INGREDIENTS:**

- ◆ 2 eggs
- ◆ Toppings of your choice

**DIRECTIONS:**

1. Spray a non-stick cooking pan with cooking spray
2. Heat the pan on a medium high heat
3. Once hot, lower the heat to medium and crack the eggs into the pan. Swirl around to evenly cover the bottom of the pan.
4. Once cooked all the way through, add your toppings (avo, veggies, turkey sausage)to the center of the mixture, and fold the edge in to cover the toppings.

Lunch : Pork Chops in Tomato Sauce (See page 34)

Dinner: Spinach and Mushroom smothered Chicken (See page 63)

# DAY 17

Breakfast: Veggie Sausage Fritatta (See page 17)

Lunch:

## *CUCUMBER FINGER SANDWICHES*

*Calories: 565*
*Carbohydrates: 26% (64.58g) | Fat: 47% (22.83) | Protein: 47% (25.4g)*

### INGREDIENTS:

- 4 slices of whole-wheat bread
- Low-fat cream cheese
- Cucumber slices
- Dill for seasoning

### DIRECTIONS:

1. Remove the crust from the 4 slices of bread
2. Spread low fat cream cheese, cucumber slices and dill over each slice
3. Make into two sandwiches and cut each sandwich into 4 quarters

Dinner: Healthy Turkey Meatballs (See page 48)
with Tomato Bruschetta (See page 51)

# DAY 18

Breakfast: Drop Scones (See page 22)

Lunch: Asian Lettuce Wraps (See page 35)

Dinner:

## *MEAL REPLACEMENT SMOOTHIE*

*Calories: 221*
*Carbohydrates: 27% (66.35g) | Fat: 53% (25.67g) | Protein: 53% (28.83g)*

### INGREDIENTS:

- ½ cup Greek yogurt
- Handful spinach
- Handful frozen cauliflower
- 250ml flax milk
- Juice from half a lemon
- Some tofu
- Cup of frozen mixed berries

### DIRECTIONS:

1. Toss everything into a blender and blend until thick and smooth

# DAY 19

Breakfast:

## *COTTAGE CHEESE*

*Calories: 103*
*Carbohydrates: 1% (3.55g) | Fat: 9% (4.52g) | Protein: 21% (11.68g)*

**INGREDIENTS:**

- ½ cup Cottage Cheese
- Salt (optional)
- Pepper (optional)
- Fruit and Nuts (optional)
- Whole grain toast (optional)
- Whole grain cereal (optional)

**DIRECTIONS:**

1. Add the cottage cheese to a bowl and serve plain or with any of the optional choices

Lunch: Veggie Tostadas (See page 28)

Dinner: Beef kebabs (See page 56)
with cauliflower rice (See page 50)

# DAY 20

Breakfast: Cinnamon Raisin Bread (See page 24)

Lunch:

## CHICKEN NOODLE SOUP

*Calories: 1107*
*Carbohydrates: 17% (41.52g) | Fat: 75% (36.44g) | Protein: 261% (142.38g)*

### INGREDIENTS:

- 2 cups of chicken broth
- 1 medium carrot, sliced
- 1 medium celery, sliced
- ¾ cup spiral noodles
- ¾ cup cooked, shredded chicken
- Spices of your choice

### DIRECTIONS:

1. Add everything to a large pot of water
2. Let it simmer until all the flavors have combined and your soup is warm

Dinner: Chili Fried Potatoes (See page 45)
and Authentic Meatloaf (See page 58)

# DAY 21

Breakfast: Mushroom Brown Rice Hash
with poached eggs (See page 26)

Lunch: Coconut Chicken Soup (See page 40)

Dinner:

## *OPEN-FACED GRILLED VEGGIE SANDWICH*

*Calories: 935*
*Carbohydrates: 54% (133.51g) | Fat: 88% (42.54g) | Protein: 33% (17.93g)*

### INGREDIENTS:

- 1 slice whole-wheat bread
- Your choice of grilled fajita veggies
- Some hummus
- Some avo
- 1 cup blueberries

### DIRECTIONS:

1. Toast the bread
2. Top with your choice of grilled fajita veggies, hummus and avo
3. Add blueberries to round out this meal

# DAY 22

Breakfast:

## WHOLEGRAIN CEREAL

*Calories:136*
*Carbohydrates: 9% (22.43g) | Fat: 6% (2.9g) | Protein: 12% (6.45g)*

**INGREDIENTS:**

- ½ cup of wholegrain cereal
- ½ cup of 2% or almond milk
- Fruits and nuts (optional)

**DIRECTIONS:**

1. Add the cereal and milk together in a bowl. Add some fruit and nuts if desired.

Lunch: Spinach rolls (See page 31)

Dinner: Coconut Chicken Soup (See page 40)
with Cumin Quick Bread (See page 47)

# DAY 23

Breakfast: Honey Grapefruit with Banana (See page 16)

Lunch:

## SNACK PACK LUNCH

*Nutritional information unavailable*

................................................................................................

### INGREDIENTS:

♦ Grab everything that needs eating in your fridge! Deli meats, cheeses, crackers, nuts, hummus, grape tomatoes, etc

### DIRECTIONS:

1. Make a charcuterie lunch with all your snacks.

Dinner: Snapper with Tomato Caper topping (See page 54)

# DAY 24

Breakfast: Crustless Ham and Asparagus Quiche (See page 18)

Lunch: Low Carb Cauliflower "Potato" salad (See page 39)

Dinner:

## QUICK PASTA SALAD

*Calories: 560*
*Carbohydrates: 29% (71.37g) | Fat: 50% (24.38g) | Protein: 32% (17.6g)*

### INGREDIENTS:

- 1 cup cold, cooked pasta
- Feta cheese
- Olives
- Chopped cherry tomatoes
- Chopped red onion
- Sliced mushrooms
- Italian dressing

### DIRECTIONS:

1. Add everything in a bowl and mix.

# DAY 25

## Breakfast:

### *SCRAMBLED EGGS AND TOAST*

*Calories: 368*
*Carbohydrates: 8% (19.93g0 | Fat: 43% (21.03g) | Protein: 43% (23.45g)*

**INGREDIENTS:**

- 2 eggs
- 1 slice whole grain toast
- Seasonings of your choice

**DIRECTIONS:**

1. Scramble 2 eggs in a non-stick pan over a medium heat
2. Seasoning as desired
3. Serve on whole grain toast

## Lunch: Healthy Stuffed Chicken Breast (See page 39)

## Dinner: Zucchini Tomato Bake (See page 62)

# DAY 26

Breakfast: Blueberry Popovers (See page 23)

Lunch:

## *PEANUT BUTTER AND BANANA SANDWICH*

*Calories: 510*
*Carbohydrates: 31% (16.01g) | Fat: 33% (16.01g) | Protein: 40% (21.57g)*

**INGREDIENTS:**

- ◆ 2 slices whole grain bread
- ◆ 2 tablespoon peanut or almond butter
- ◆ 1 banana

**DIRECTIONS:**

1. Combine two slices of whole grain bread with your choice of nut butter and one banana, sliced over entire sandwich.

Dinner: Prosciutto Wrapped Chicken Breast (See page 61) with Potato Cakes (See page 46)

# DAY 27

Breakfast: Applesauce Pancakes (See page 15)

Lunch: Barley and Black Bean Salad (See page 37)

Dinner:

## BAKED POTATO

*Calories: 284*
*Carbohydrates: 26% (64.46g) | Fat: 1% (0.33g) | Protein: 14% (7.45g)*

### INGREDIENTS:

- 1 medium potato
- Any toppings of your choice.

### DIRECTIONS:

1. Wash and poke holes in the potato with a fork
2. Microwave for around 7 minutes or until soft to the touch. Allow to cool
3. Slice, mash the middle and top with your choice of toppings, like Greek yogurt, low-fat cream cheese, etc.

# DAY 28

Breakfast:

## *ALMONDS AND FRUITS*

*Calories: 500*
*Carbohydrates: 13% (32.71g) | Fat: 78% (37.7g) | Protein: 30% (16.35g)*

**INGREDIENTS:**

- ◆ Handful of raw almonds
- ◆ Handful low glycemic fruits

**DIRECTIONS:**

1. A great on-the-go meal! A handful of raw almonds with some blueberries, an apple, or an orange make a quick and easy filling breakfast.

Lunch: Beef Fajitas (See page 33)

Dinner: Marinated Turkey Breast (See page 60)
with Tomato Bruschetta (See page 51)

# DAY 29

Breakfast: Honey Grapefruit with Banana (See page 16)

Lunch: Three Pepper Pizza (See page 29)

Dinner:

## *VEGGIE PASTA*

*Calories: 478*
*Carbohydrates: 40% (97.71g) | Fat: 10% (4.92g) | Protein: 33% (17.86g)*

### INGREDIENTS:

- 1 cup whole-wheat pasta
- ½ cup mixed chopped veggies (frozen)
- ½ cup marinara sauce
- 1 teaspoon minced garlic
- Salt and Pepper

### DIRECTIONS:

1. Defrost some mixed chopped veggies in a medium saucepan over a medium heat
2. Add the marinara sauce, minced garlic, salt and pepper
3. Pour over cooked whole wheat pasta and serve warm

# DAY 30

Breakfast: Veggie Sausage Frittata (See page 17)

Lunch:

## HUMMUS PLATTER

*Calories: 889*
*Carbohydrates: 47% (115.96g) | Fat: 81% (39.3g) | Protein: 36% (19.48g)*

### INGREDIENTS:

- ◆ 1 tin hummus (or make your own)
- ◆ Chopped carrots
- ◆ Chopped bell peppers
- ◆ Chopped celery
- ◆ Handful tortilla chips

### DIRECTIONS:

1. Combine everything on a cheese board and dip into the hummus

Dinner: Basil Scallops with Spinach Fettucine (See page 55)

Printed in Great Britain
by Amazon